To My Daughter

Compiled by
Lois L. Kaufman

Design by
Scharr Design

PETER PAUPER PRESS, INC.
WHITE PLAINS · NEW YORK

For Ellen

CONTENTS

DAUGHTERS

Oh my son's my son till he gets him a wife,
But my daughter's my daughter all her life.
DINAH MARIA MULOCK CRAIK

My mother wanted me to be her wings, to fly
as she never quite had the courage to do. I
love her for that. I love the fact that she
wanted to give birth to her own wings.
ERICA JONG

Thou art thy mother's glass, and she in thee
Calls back the lovely April of her prime.
SHAKESPEARE

We are together, my child and I. Mother and
child, yes, but *sisters* really, against whatever
denies us all that we are.
ALICE WALKER

Never grow a wishbone, daughter, where your backbone ought to be.

CLEMENTINE PADDLEFORD

My mother won't admit it, but I've always been a disappointment to her. Deep down inside, she'll never forgive herself for giving birth to a daughter who refuses to launder aluminum foil and use it over again.

ERMA BOMBECK

She tried in every way to understand me, and she succeeded. It was this deep, loving understanding as long as she lived that more than anything else helped and sustained me on my way to success.

MAE WEST

My mother was dead for five years before I knew that I had loved her very much.

LILLIAN HELLMAN

Misery is when you make your bed and then your mother tells you it's the day she's changing the sheets.

SUZANNE HELLER

Who ran to help me when I fell,
And would some pretty story tell,
Or kiss the place to make it well?
  My Mother.

ANN TAYLOR

To me the only answer a woman can make to the destructive forces of the world is creation. And the most ecstatic form of creation is the creation of new life.

JESSIE BERNARD,
to her unborn daughter

Most of us become parents long before we have stopped being children.

MIGNON MCLAUGHLIN

I hid myself within myself, I only considered myself and quietly wrote down all my joys, sorrows and contempt in my diary . . . I used to be furious with Mummy, and still am sometimes. It's true that she doesn't understand me, but I don't understand her either.

ANNE FRANK

My earliest memories were of my mother writing her PhD dissertation and taking care of my brother and myself. Her emphasis on education, social responsibility, and the importance of a woman's fulfilling herself have shaped my outlook fundamentally and irrevocably.

ELIZABETH HOLTZMAN

If I had another child—I'd like a girl—I can't say just how I'd raise her, but one thing I can tell you is that she will not be spoiled. The whole thing is about earning your own way and you don't really get there until you earn it. That's the real truth.

TINA TURNER

A mother is not a person to lean on, but a person to make leaning unnecessary.

DOROTHY CANFIELD FISHER

... But mothers can't give the world (nor fathers, nor even husbands, lovers or children)—the world sometimes just happens to us.

ANNE SEXTON,
to her daughter Linda

There's nothing wrong with teenagers that reasoning with them won't aggravate.

ANONYMOUS

Long before she was born, I tried to influence her future life by association with music, art, and natural beauty. Perhaps this prenatal preparation helped make Shirley what she is today.

SHIRLEY TEMPLE'S MOTHER

Likely as not, the child you can do the least
with will do the most to make you proud.

MIGNON MCLAUGHLIN

It is the privilege of adults to give advice. It is
the privilege of youth not to listen. Both avail
themselves of their privileges, and the world
rocks along.

D. SUTTEN

With girls, everything looks great on the
surface. But beware of drawers that won't
open. They contain a three-month supply of
dirty underwear, unwashed hose, and rubber
bands with blobs of hair in them.

ERMA BOMBECK

A daughter is the companion, the friend, and
confidant of her mother, and the object of a
pleasure something like the love between
the angels to her father.

RICHARD STEELE

12

Everything you are and do from fifteen to eighteen is what you are and will do through life.

SCOTT FITZGERALD,
letter to his daughter

I have so many anxieties about her growing up. I just hope she will get a chance to grow up. I hope there's a world for her to grow up in. I watch the news and I think, " . . . they're going to blow up the world, just when I've got this little peach here."

MERYL STREEP

The children despise their parents until the age of forty, when they suddenly become just like them—thus preserving the system.

QUENTIN CREWE

The heart of a mother is a deep abyss at the bottom of which you will always discover forgiveness.

HONORE DE BALZAC

13

How precious your motherhood is as I think what blessing you have helped to bring to mothers all over the world. Here is a treasure of comfort for you to lay up in your heart on your birthday.

HELEN KELLER,
to her mother

In a child's lunch basket, a mother's thoughts.

JAPANESE PROVERB

In giving our daughter life, her father and I had also given her death, something I hadn't realized until that new creature flailed her arms in what was now infinite space. We had given her disease and speeding cars and flying cornices: once out of the fortress that had been myself, she would never be safe again. . . . We disappoint our kids and they disappoint us, and sometimes they grow up into people we don't like very much. We go on loving, though what we love may be more memory than actuality. And until the day we die we fear the phone that rings in the middle of the night.

MARY CANTWELL

What the daughter does, the mother did.

JEWISH PROVERB

In intimate family life, there comes a
moment when children, willingly or no,
become the judges of their parents.

HONORE DE BALZAC

If one has plenty of money, but no children,
he cannot be reckoned rich: if one has
children, but no money, he cannot be
considered poor.

CHINESE PROVERB

I stopped believing in Santa Claus when I
was six. Mother took me to see him in a
department store and he asked for my
autograph.

SHIRLEY TEMPLE

Mummy herself has told us that she looked upon us more as her friends than her daughters. Now that is all very fine, but still, a friend can't take a mother's place. I need my mother as an example which I can follow.

ANNE FRANK

I spent hours rummaging through my mother's drawers, dabbing her cologne behind my ears, putting on her rhinestone earrings, reading anniversary cards my father had given her, sifting through the hodgepodge in her pocketbooks. I was hunting for clues about what it was to be a woman. I was searching for some secret I knew she had, but wouldn't willingly share with me.

ANGELA BARRON MCBRIDE

I think a parent is always tougher on a child of the same sex—because they're *us*. Vanessa is exactly me: stubborn, independent-minded, emotional, quixotic, moody—and lacking in confidence.

JANE FONDA

There are many things I will never forgive my mother for, but heading the list is the fact that she did the Double-Crostic in ink.

NORA EPHRON

At the moment that a boy of thirteen is turning towards girls, a girl of thirteen is turning on her mother. This girl can get rather unreasonable, often saying such comical things as, "Listen, this is my life!"

BILL COSBY

Mothers and daughters are not only natural allies; they are natural enemies. They are at odds for the attentions of the men in their families—fathers, husbands, sons, brothers— just as women are often at odds for the attentions of men anywhere. Families are basic training ground for the combat of later life.

LIZ SMITH

Probably there is nothing in human nature more resonant with charges than the flow of energy between two biologically alike bodies, one of which has lain in amniotic bliss inside the other, one of which has labored to give birth to the other.

ADRIENNE RICH

It is not a bad thing that children should occasionally, and politely, put parents in their place.

COLETTE

All women become like their mothers. That is their tragedy. No man does. That's his.

OSCAR WILDE

"Equal parenting" does not work—the maternal tuning in never turns off.

PHYLLIS SCHLAFLY

Whatever beauty or poetry is to be found in my little book is owing to your interest in and encouragement of all my efforts from the first to the last; and if ever I do anything to be proud of, my greatest happiness will be that I can thank you for that, as I may do for all the good there is in me; and I shall be content to write if it gives you pleasure.

LOUISA MAY ALCOTT,
to her mother

I never thought she'd turn on me. When I was sinking in a sea of diapers, formulas and congenital spitting, Mother couldn't wait to pull her grandchildren onto her lap and say, "Let me tell you how rotten your mommy was. She never took naps, and she never picked up her room, and she had a mouth like a drunken sailor in Shanghai. I washed her mouth out with soap so many times I finally had to starch her tongue."

ERMA BOMBECK

Creative minds always have been known to survive any kind of bad training.

ANNA FREUD

THE CHILDREN'S HOUR

Between the dark and the daylight,
    When the night is beginning to lower,
Comes a pause in the day's occupation,
    That is known as the Children's Hour.

I hear in the chamber above me
    The patter of little feet,
The sound of a door that is opened,
    And voices soft and sweet.

From my study I see in the lamplight,
    Descending the broad hall stair,
Grave Alice, and laughing Allegra,
    And Edith with golden hair.

A whisper, and then a silence:
    Yet I know by their merry eyes
They are plotting and planning together
    To take me by surprise.

A sudden rush from the stairway,
    A sudden raid from the hall!
By three doors left unguarded
    They enter my castle wall!

They climb up into my turret
 O'er the arms and back of my chair;
If I try to escape, they surround me;
 They seem to be everywhere.

They almost devour me with kisses,
 Their arms about me entwine,
Till I think of the Bishop of Bingen
 In his Mouse-Tower on the Rhine!

Do you think, O blue-eyed banditti,
 Because you have scaled the wall,
Such an old mustache as I am
 Is not a match for you all!

I have you fast in my fortress,
 And will not let you depart,
But put you down into the dungeon
 In the round-tower of my heart.

And there will I keep you forever,
 Yes, forever and a day,
Till the wall shall crumble to ruin,
 And moulder in dust away.
     HENRY WADSWORTH LONGFELLOW

I remember a time when I marched into Katherine Josephine's room and pretended to be surprised to discover that somebody was occupying the bassinet. "Don't tell me that *you're* still here!" I exclaimed. "Listen, kid, do you know what day it is? It's the ninth, you're four months old, and you're not getting any younger, let me tell you. These are your best months and what are you doing with them? Nothing. For your information, babies a lot smaller than you are already out advertising North Star Blankets and you just lie here fluttering your fingers.

JEAN KERR

Things change so fast, you can't use 1971 ethics on someone born in 1971. Whatever she does is going to look far-out to me. I hope I'll either like it or keep my mouth shut.

GRACE SLICK,
about her infant daughter

Your mother's always wrong; that's why they made her your mother.

BRUCE JAY FRIEDMAN

Women know
The way to rear up children (to be just),
They know a merry, simple, tender knack
Of tying sashes, fitting babies' shoes,
And stringing pretty words that make no
    sense,
And kissing full sense into empty words;
Which things are corals to cut life upon
Although such trifles.

ELIZABETH BARRETT BROWNING
from Aurora Leigh

There was a little girl,
Who had a little curl
Right in the middle of her forehead;
And when she was good
She was very, very good,
But when she was bad she was horrid.

HENRY WADSWORTH LONGFELLOW

Girls mature faster than boys, cost more to raise, and statistics show that the old saw about girls not knowing about money and figures is a myth. Girls start to outspend boys before puberty—and they manage to maintain this lead until death or an ugly credit manager, whichever comes first. . . . Girls can slam a door louder, beg longer, turn tears on and off like a faucet, and invented the term, "You don't trust me."

ERMA BOMBECK

Spock, shlock, don't talk to me about that stuff. A man doesn't know how to bring up children until he's been a mother.

DAN GREENBURG

The generation of daughters now growing up may be the first one in history to feel that motherhood can be one choice among many that a woman can make.

SIGNE HAMMER

As a little girl I had a very strong drive to be a mother. It's what I wanted more than anything else. I was very attached to my dolls—I had six of them—and I used to line them up in bed next to me. I was so busy making sure that they weren't going to be smothered that I couldn't sleep. . . . I had to take very good care of my dolls. I knew my mother was doing it wrong, and I figured I could do it better.

BEATRICE SCHWARTZ

I hardly remember her, but I have missed her all my life.

BARBARA HUTTON,
about her dead mother

You do *need* certain limits, rules, despite the fact that you are 18 and in many, many ways a grown woman and want to burst forth upon the world and be free . . . freedom comes from within and with it comes many responsibilities, and restrictions that YOU must set for yourself.

ANNE SEXTON,
to her daughter Joy

MEN

Plain women know more about men than beautiful ones do.

KATHARINE HEPBURN

Before marriage, a man declares that he would lay down his life to serve you; after marriage, he won't even lay down his newspaper to talk to you.

HELEN ROWLAND

A man is always afraid of a woman who loves him too well.

JOHN GAY

I like a man who talks me to death, provided he is amusing; it saves so much trouble.

MARY SHELLEY

I like men to behave like men—strong and childish.

FRANCOISE SAGAN

I should like to see any kind of a man, distinguishable from a gorilla, that some good and even pretty woman could not shape a husband out of.

OLIVER WENDELL HOLMES

Being a woman is a terribly difficult task, since it consists principally in dealing with men.

JOSEPH CONRAD

If you want to know what a man is really like, take notice how he acts when he loses money.

NEW ENGLAND PROVERB

American women expect to find in their husbands a perfection that English women only hope to find in their butlers.

W. SOMERSET MAUGHAM

I refuse to consign the whole male sex to the nursery. I insist on believing that some men are my equals.

BRIGID BROPHY

It is interesting to know that most Cambridge boys preferred me when I was sick with sinus and they could take care of me, because that was the only time they were stronger.

SYLVIA PLATH

The best way to find out if a man has done something is to advise him to do it. He will not be able to resist boasting that he has done it without being advised.

COMTESSE DIANE

It's not the men in my life that counts—it's the life in my men.

MAE WEST

Most hierarchies were established by men who now monopolize the upper levels, thus depriving women of their rightful share of opportunities for incompetence.

LAURENCE PETER

Success has made failures of many men.

CINDY ADAMS

Sigh no more, ladies, sigh no more.
Men were deceivers ever;
One foot in sea, and one on shore;
To one thing constant never.

SHAKESPEARE

There will be some men who under no circumstances can allow a woman to pay a check. By all means, allow him to pay for his own outdated view of chivalry.

DEE WEDEMEYER

The best man for a man and the best man for a woman are not the same.

JOSE ORTEGA Y GASSET

I love men, not because they are men, but because they are not women.

CHRISTINA, QUEEN OF SWEDEN

They say best men are molded out of faults,
And, for the most, become much more the
   better
For being a little bad.

SHAKESPEARE

Whatever women do they must do twice as well as men to be thought half as good. Luckily, this is not difficult.

CHARLOTTE WHITTON

Fortune does not change men; it unmasks them.

MADAME SUZANNE NECKER

First time you buy a house you see how pretty the paint is and buy it. The second time you look to see if the basement has termites. It's the same with men.

LUPE VELEZ

The men that women marry,
And why they marry them, will always be
A marvel and a mystery to the world.

HENRY WADSWORTH LONGFELLOW

Sexiness wears thin after a while and beauty
fades, but to be married to a man who makes
you laugh every day, ah, now that's a real
treat!

JOANNE WOODWARD

Woman is stronger by virtue of her feelings
than man by virtue of his power.

HONORE DE BALZAC

WOMEN

I see all the young women having the same anxieties about men I did. That doesn't change.

HELEN GURLEY BROWN

In nine cases out of ten, a woman had better show more affection than she feels.

JANE AUSTEN

God did not create woman from man's head, that he should command her, nor from his feet, that she should be his slave, but rather from his side, that she should be near his heart.

TALMUD

A woman is the only thing I am afraid of that I know won't hurt me.

ABRAHAM LINCOLN

To educate a man is to form an individual who leaves nothing behind him; to educate a woman is to form future generations.

EDOUARD LEBOULAYE

A woman has to sacrifice all claims to femininity and family to be a writer.

SYLVIA PLATH

No person should be denied equal rights because of the shape of her skin.

PATRICK PAULSEN

I thought that we would wake up this morning and have the same rights as our husbands, grandsons and garbagemen—but we are still begging to be let into our country's Constitution.

LIZ CARPENTER, *1979*

If you're not beguiling by age twelve, forget it.

LUCY,
Peanuts

My grandmother wanted to live long enough to vote for a woman president. I'll be satisfied if I live to see a woman go before the Supreme Court and hear the justices acknowledge, "Gentlemen, she's human. She deserves the protection of our laws."

MARTHA WRIGHT GRIFFITHS

A woman's guess is much more accurate than a man's certainty.

RUDYARD KIPLING

No matter how happily a woman may be married, it always pleases her to discover that there is a nice man who wishes she were not.

H. L. MENCKEN

The years that a woman subtracts from her age are not lost. They are added to the ages of other women.

DIANE DE POITIERS

The difference between us is very marked. Most that I have done has been in public and I have received much encouragement at every step of the way. You, on the other hand, have labored in a private way. I have wrought in the day, and you in the night. I have had the applause of the crowd and the satisfaction that comes of being approved by the multitude, while the most that you have done has been witnessed by a few trembling . . . bondsmen and women . . . whose heartfelt "God bless you" has been your only reward.

FREDERICK DOUGLASS,
to Harriet Tubman

A lady's imagination is very rapid; it jumps from admiration to love, from love to matrimony, in a moment.

JANE AUSTEN

To feel, to love, to suffer and to devote herself will always be the text of a woman's life.

HONORE DE BALZAC

When I see the elaborate study and ingenuity displayed by women in the pursuit of trifles, I feel no doubt of their capacity for the most Herculean undertakings.

JULIA WARD HOWE

Without the women's movement, how many of us could have had the strength to change our own lives?

BETTY FRIEDAN

If you scratch a homemaker, you'll find a feminist one eighth of an inch from the surface.

LETTY COTTIN POGREBIN

With these activities came opportunity to know women who shared my conviction that there is so much women can do in the modern world and should be permitted to do irrespective of sex. Probably my greatest satisfaction was to indicate by example now and then, that women can sometimes do things themselves if given the chance.

AMELIA EARHART

The heart may think it knows better: the senses know that absence blots people out.

ELIZABETH BOWEN

No frozen-hearted woman ever I laid eyes on but has made duty her religion.

HONORE DE BALZAC

I think that implicit in the women's movement is the idea that women will share in the economic burden, and men will share more equally in the home and the family.

BETTY FRIEDAN

We did not labor in suffrage just to bring the vote to women but to allow women to express their opinions and become effective in government.

JEANNETTE RANKIN

From birth to age 18, a girl needs good parents, from 18 to 35 she needs good looks, from 35 to 55 she needs a good personality, and from 55 on she needs cash.

SOPHIE TUCKER

One should never trust a woman who tells one her real age. A woman who would tell that would tell anything.

OSCAR WILDE

Love is a capricious creature which desires everything and can be contented with almost nothing.

MADELEINE DE SCUDERY

LOVE AND MARRIAGE

No woman sleeps so soundly that the twang
of a guitar will not bring her to the window.

SPANISH PROVERB

I hope I showed you that loving means
letting go too. Letting go of NEEDING to be
loved, and simply loving. It's somewhat like
the way you girls tend your plants. Their
response is born of your initial actions. Love
blooms that way too. When we love, we
become loved.

ISA KOGON,
to her daughters

To love is to find pleasure in the happiness of
the person loved.

LEIBNITZ

Love is having somebody to nudge when you
see something you like and want to share it.

UNKNOWN

The more you judge, the less you love.

HONORE DE BALZAC

Among even the happiest married couples
there are always moments of regret.

HONORE DE BALZAC

Love which is only an episode in the life of
men, is the entire history of the life of
women.

MADAME DE STAEL

We should place our aspirations and our
dreams very high—and I also think it is a
source of disappointment to make all the
interest of one's life depend on sentiments as
stormy as love.

MARIE CURIE,
to her daughter Eve

Friendship is like being comfortably filled with roast beef; love, like being enlivened with champagne.

SAMUEL JOHNSON

When two people are under the influence of the most violent, most insane, most delusive, and most transient of passions, they are required to swear that they will remain in that excited, abnormal, and exhausting condition continuously until death do them part.

GEORGE BERNARD SHAW

A good husband is a plaster that cures all the ills of girlhood.

MOLIERE

To be emotionally committed to somebody is very difficult, but to be alone is impossible.

STEPHEN SONDHEIM

The vow of fidelity is an absurd commitment, but it is the heart of marriage.

FATHER ROBERT CAPON

Marrying a man is like buying something you've been admiring for a long time in a shop window. You may love it when you get it home, but it doesn't always go with everything else in the house.

JEAN KERR

Husbands are like fires. They go out if unattended.

ZSA ZSA GABOR

A sound marriage is not based on complete frankness; it is based on a sensible reticence.

MORRIS L. ERNST

A deaf husband and a blind wife are always a happy couple.

DANISH PROVERB

Marriage is a fight to the death. Before contracting it, the two parties concerned implore the benediction of Heaven because to promise to love each other forever is the rashest of enterprises.

HONORE DE BALZAC

Love sought is good, but given unsought, is better.

SHAKESPEARE

Remember very slight things make epochs in married life.

GEORGE ELIOT

Subduing and subdued, the petty strife,
Which clouds the colour of domestic life;
The sober comfort, all the peace which
    springs
From the large aggregate of little things;
On these small cares of daughter, wife or
    friend,
The almost sacred joys of home depend.

HANNAH MORE

I had always thought that marriage represented
a distinct change in one's life, with always
the lurking possibility that one might
suddenly awake to the fact that the change
was not agreeable at all. Instead I have found
it just a delightful continuation of a rare and
beautiful comradeship.

LELLA SECOR,
World War I journalist

How do you know that love is gone? If you
said you would be there by seven, you get
there by nine, and he or she has not called
the police yet—it's gone.

MARLENE DIETRICH

Love, *n.* A temporary insanity curable by marriage or by removal of the patient from the influences under which he incurred the disorder. This disease, like *caries* and many other ailments, is prevalent only among civilized races living under artificial conditions; barbarous nations breathing pure air and eating simple food enjoy immunity from its ravages. It is sometimes fatal, but more frequently to the physician than to the patient.

AMBROSE BIERCE

Keep thy eyes open before marriage; and half shut afterwards.

THOMAS FULLER

Often the difference between a successful marriage and a mediocre one consists of leaving about three or four things a day unsaid.

HARLAN MILLER

Marriage is an edifice that must be rebuilt every day.

ANDRE MAUROIS

I have lived long enough to know that the evening glow of love has its own riches and splendour.

BENJAMIN DISRAELI

A marriage is like a long trip in a tiny rowboat: if one passenger starts to rock the boat, the other has to steady it; otherwise they will go to the bottom together.

DAVID REUBEN

Love must be learned, and learned again and again; there is no end to it. Hate needs no instruction, but waits only to be provoked.

KATHERINE ANN PORTER

We would have broken up except for the children. Who were the children? Well, she and I were.

MORT SAHL

A dress that zips up the back will bring a husband and wife together.

JAMES H. BOREN

Marriageable girls as well as mothers understand the terms and perils of the lottery called wedlock. That is why women weep at a wedding and men smile.

HONORE DE BALZAC

A woman knows the face of the man she loves as a sailor knows the open sea.

HONORE DE BALZAC

Men are April when they woo, December
when they wed: maids are May when they
are maids, but the sky changes when they are
wives.

SHAKESPEARE

The sound of a kiss is not so loud as that of a
cannon, but its echo lasts a great deal longer.

OLIVER WENDELL HOLMES

O the pleasure of counting the melancholy
clock by a snoring husband!

GEORGE FARQUHAR

A husband must never fall asleep before his
wife or awaken after her.

HONORE DE BALZAC

Almost all married people fight, although many are ashamed to admit it. Actually a marriage in which no quarreling at all takes place may well be one that is dead or dying from emotional undernourishment. If you care, you probably fight.

FLORA DAVIS

LIFE

There is nothing in life except what we put into it.

MADAME SCHWETCHINE

The true way of softening one's troubles is to solace those of others.

MADAME DE MAINTENON

Life would be infinitely happier if we could only be born at the age of eighty and gradually approach eighteen.

MARK TWAIN

The power to animate all of life's seasons is a power that resides within us.

GAIL SHEEHY

Life resembles a novel more often than
novels resemble life.

GEORGE SAND

I wish I knew what people meant when they
say they find "emptiness" in this wonderful
adventure of living, which seems to me to
pile up its glories like an horizon-wide sunset
as the light declines. I'm afraid I'm an
incorrigible life-lover, life-wonderer, and
adventurer.

EDITH WHARTON

Youth is a disease from which we all recover.

DOROTHY FULDHEIM

Misfortune, no less than happiness, inspires
us to dream.

HONORE DE BALZAC

It is of great importance in a republic not only to guard against the oppression of its rulers, but to guard one part of society against the injustice of the other part.

ALEXANDER HAMILTON

A touch of folly is needed if we are to extricate ourselves successfully from some of the hazards of life.

LA ROCHEFOUCAULD

As long as I have a want, I have a reason for living. Satisfaction is death.

GEORGE BERNARD SHAW

Endurance is frequently a form of indecision.

ELIZABETH BIBESCO

The most fatal illusion is the settled point of view. Since life is growth and motion, a fixed point of view kills anybody who has one.

BROOKS ATKINSON

The world is a comedy to those who think and a tragedy to those who feel.

HORACE WALPOLE

What we call progress is the exchange of one nuisance for another nuisance.

Attributed to HAVELOCK ELLIS

Parables are unnecessary for recognizing the blatant absurdity of everyday life. Reality is lesson enough.

JANE O'REILLY

Our greatest happiness . . . does not depend on the condition of life in which chance has placed us, but is always the result of a good conscience, good health, occupation, and freedom in all just pursuits.

THOMAS JEFFERSON

The greatest pleasure I have known is to do a good action by stealth, and to have it found out by accident.

CHARLES LAMB

Success, *n.* The one unpardonable sin against one's fellows.

AMBROSE BIERCE

A man must learn to endure patiently that which he cannot avoid conveniently.

MICHEL DE MONTAIGNE

Life is a hospital, in which every patient is possessed by the desire of changing his bed. One would prefer to suffer near the fire, and another is certain that he would get well if he were by the window.

CHARLES BAUDELAIRE

There is no cure for birth and death save to enjoy the interval.

GEORGE SANTAYANA

Experience is a good teacher, but she sends in terrific bills.

MINNA ANTRIM

Experience is the name everyone gives to their mistakes.

OSCAR WILDE

Inspiration comes of working every day.

CHARLES BAUDELAIRE

A moment's insight is sometimes worth a
life's experience.

OLIVER WENDELL HOLMES

Let us be kind, if we wish to be regretted.

PIERRE LOTI

Life is the art of drawing sufficient
conclusions from insufficient premises.

SAMUEL BUTLER

Joy is the feeling that comes from fulfillment
of one's potential.

WILLIAM C. SCHUTZ

Living is a form of not being sure, not knowing what next or how.

AGNES DE MILLE

Our chief want in life is somebody who will make us do what we can.

RALPH WALDO EMERSON

There are moments when everything goes well; don't be frightened, it won't last.

JULES RENARD

Nothing has a stronger influence psychologically on their environment, and especially on their children, than the unlived life of the parents.

C. G. JUNG

Existence is no more than a flaw in the perfection of nonexistence.

PAUL VALERY

Execute every act of thy life as though it were thy last.

MARCUS AURELIUS

Not to do honor to old age is to demolish in the morning the house wherein we are to sleep at night.

ALPHONSE KARR

Bloom where you are planted.

ELLA GRASSO

A MOTHER'S REFLECTIONS:
Advice to a Daughter

Be gentle.

Be kind.

Enjoy life.

Be tolerant.

*Keep a sense of humor about yourself
and the rest of the world.*

Work hard, but play hard too.

Believe in yourself.

Act on your convictions.

Be generous with your love.

Call home once a week.